Christophe Levenson

D1248067

smoked
glass

smoked glass

alden nowlan

clarke, irwin & company limited
toronto/vancouver

smoked
glass

alden
nowlan

clarke, irwin & company limited
toronto/vancouver

Canadian Cataloguing in Publication Data

Nowlan, Alden, 1933-
  Smoked glass

Poems.
ISBN 0-7720-1194-X

I. Title.

PS8527.084S66   C811'.5'4   C77-001524-7
PR9199.3.N68S66

© 1977 by Clarke, Irwin & Company Limited

ISBN 0-7720-1194-X

1 2 3 4 5 81 80 79 78 77

Printed in Canada

for claudine and johnnie
and to bert burgoyne

acknowledgements

CANADIAN LITERATURE
CROSS COUNTRY
EAST OF CANADA
EXILE
FIDDLEHEAD
52 PICKUP
4th ESTATE
INSCAPE
JEWISH DIALOGUE
PRAIRIE SCHOONER
RUNE
SATURDAY NIGHT
VENTURE

alphabetical list of poems

smoked
glass

I store a tube of tears in my refrigerator.
Many people must do the same.
It has been an excessively dry summer
and you use your eyes more than is good
for them, the doctor said.
At the drug store I was embarrassed
to see what it was
that he had prescribed for me.
Tears! Why, good God, I mean
I cry almost every day of my life.
If I've no better reason
I've only to relax my grip
to have my eyes moisten
at the memory of certain
scenes in old movies:
say, Gregory Peck's funeral
in The Gunfighter. Surely,
that ought to be enough.
I was tempted to say this
to the clerk when she handed over
the medication. Lady, it's not
what you think, my heart isn't
made of flint; believe me,
I hurt too. But that wasn't as bad
as reading the fine print
when I got home. Keep tightly
sealed and refrigerate
after use, it said.
If we have house guests I'll hide
the tube at the bottom of
the vegetable crisper.
And to think there are factories!
I picture them as being
windowless, lit by pale blue bulbs,
and containing row upon row
of workers in smocks and hairnets
who sit on long benches, bend
over long tables,
weeping into sterile tissues
for forty hours a week,
men and women who when they're asked
their occupation have to answer:
tear-maker.

4   On being detested by a friend

I know of only one person I like
who detests me. There could be others.

I like him better
each time I learn
that he's tried again
to injure me.

He does it so clumsily
it's obvious he's never
done it to anyone before

and afterwards he
despises himself;
his grin is ghastly
with guilt when we

come face to face
and must talk.
This happens
once or twice a month:
ours is a small city.

I don't think he knows
that I know he detests me
but I'm almost sure
he knows I like him

and is miserable
because of this.

I wonder if there's
anyone I detest
who likes me?
I think I would like him.

It is not elephants. I would not laugh at them
as I climbed the fire ladder to the moored balloon
and the rungs turned into broom straw and I fell
towards their tusks and the crocodiles. But I would forget
as soon as it was over and I home, here in my bed.
It is not elephants, nor are there snakes and spiders.
Nothing like that. The setting is always
one with which I'm familiar or, rather, it combines
people I've known and places I've been
in curious ways. A house will have been moved
hundreds of miles and contain rooms from another
house or apartment; and people I knew
when I was a child and never saw again
will be in partnership with others
I've met only this year. A professor of English
and a physician will be running a shoe factory
where I used to work but in a different town.
The past will have been altered
in ways that matter greatly only to me:
the woman to whom I'm married is not
the woman I married but another I might have
married, and I know this. And something is required of me
—now we've come to it—something is required of me,
something in my line of work, or there's some test
I must pass, there's always something I have to
do, something I must do if life is to continue
to be worth living, something I've done before
or very much like something
I've done before. And I can't. Oh, I can almost
do it, that's the worst of it, I have it almost
within my grasp. But I can't. And it takes a long time
to wake up, it takes a very long time to wake up,
because I'm not asleep, you see, this is different
from being asleep. No, it is not elephants.

The world is gone mad
at (what time is it?)
4 a.m.
          Huh, what kind of man
believing he hears
something monstrous
happening just outside
turns first to his watch?
          A schizophrenic
reporter, me,
yanked away by the screams
of two small children
fighting in the dark,
babies
who've crawled here
from God knows where
to fight and are
screaming horribly.

They're cats, of course.
But I've got to stop it
—not the fight,
but the sound of it.
Got to.
          I hiss
from my bedroom
window and they
scatter, one
through the tall grass, one
into the bushes.
          Afterwards
I go down and let Hodge in.
She looks like
a particular kind
of human being,
a respectable person
who has done something
crazy in public
for the first time
and knows he'll do it again.

Old cat, you make me
uncomfortable
in this strange,
dead of the night kitchen.
You could kill me easily,
couldn't you, although I'm so big
and you're so small, attack me in my sleep.

And when I tell this
at breakfast, with sunflowers
on the table and fresh
strawberries,
     Claudine says
she's thought, once or twice,
no more than that,
about the two-year-olds
with whom she works,
of how much violence
there is in them,
of how the eighteen,
if they came at her
all at once, could
beat and bite her
to death in minutes,
if only they knew it.

In the garden

"When I die
I'll grow wings
and fly.

   Don't grin,"

said the caterpillar,
crawling by.

8   Full circle

In my youth, no one spoke of love
where I lived, except I spoke of it,
and then only in the dark. The word was known
like the name of a city on another continent.
No one called anyone his friend,
although they had friends. Perhaps they were afraid
to commit so much of themselves,
to demand so much of others; for if they'd said,
"We're friends," as they never did,
it would have been a contract.
As it was, they could quarrel,
even hit one another if they were drunk,
and remain friends, never having said it.
Where nothing was sworn there could be no betrayal.
Nor did they touch
casually; their persons seemed to occupy
more space than their bodies did.
Seeing an adult run we'd have looked first for the reason
in the direction from which he came. We never met trains;
my people were like that.
                              It was not enough for me.
"I love you," I said.
Whispered it, painfully, and was laughed at;
hid until the wounds healed and said it again,
          muttered it.
Wanting to be loved, "I love you," was what I said.
And I learned to touch, as a legless man
learns to walk again.
                    Came to live among people
who called anyone a friend
who was not an enemy, to whom there were no strangers:
because there were so many, they were invisible.
Now, like everyone else, I send
postcards to acquaintances, With Love—
Love meaning, I suppose, that I remember the recipients
kindly and wish them well. But I say it
less often and will not be surprised
at myself if the time comes when I do not say it,
when I do not touch, except desperately, when I ask
nothing more of others, but greet them with a wink,
as my grandfather might have done, looking up
for an instant from his carpenter's bench.

9   **There was a time when children died**

We knew there'd been a time when children died.
Every old person in our settlement
possessed a brother or a sister who
would never age. Those small Victorians,
the boys in stockings and the girls in frocks
that bent the grass, had chased their barrel hoops
and spun their tops the day before; their names
were those we answered to; they ran beside us,
not knowing what we knew. Diphtheria
or typhoid, one of those plagues (cholera
being another) which sound so much like
a witch's synonyms for Satan, had
their throats between its thumbs and soon the lamp
would rise and float above the table, whirl
until the house was whirling, too, and then
go out and leave such darkness that they'd try
to find their hands and couldn't. Aubrey, Clare,
Amantha, little ones who might have been
my great aunts and great uncles but instead
were almost playmates of that bare-kneed boy
who lives on only as a ghost in me.

10 The visitor

Last summer we found a sleeping bag
in our back yard, under the cedars
where we don't mow the grass.
Someone had slept there.

A friend had arrived late
the previous night, we decided,
and hadn't wanted to wake us.
He'd got up early and gone
to see someone else.

We stayed home all day and waited for him.

But nobody came. And the sleeping bag
was still there next morning
although it hadn't been slept in:
you can tell a bed that's been used
recently from one that hasn't
been—the disorder of
the former is in sharper focus.

Should we have brought it inside?
Should we have called the police
on the second day or the third
or the fourth? Perhaps. As it was
we forgot about it

until this spring
when we crammed it into a garbage can.
I think it was its rottenness, the sick
feel of it in my hands
that made me believe something
horrible could have happened
to whoever it was
that lay down that night
on the ground within fifty feet
of our house, just outside the light
from the bulb above the back door

or, if nothing harmed him,
that he ran away,
that young man with terrible eyes,
because he wasn't sure he could resist
temptation a second night:
for he must have watched us,
moving about the kitchen,
sitting down to dinner,
getting ready for bed,

he could have attacked us while we slept,
and how can we be sure he won't come back?

"Once when we were hunting cattle
            on the barrens,"
so began many of the stories they told,
gathered in the kitchen, a fire still
            the focus of life then,
the teapot on the stove as long as
            anyone was awake,
mittens and socks left to thaw on
            the open oven door,
chunks of pine and birch piled
            halfway to the ceiling,
and always a faint smell of smoke
            like spice in the air,
the lamps making their peace with
            the darkness,
the world not entirely answerable
            to man.

They took turns talking, the listeners
            puffed their pipes,
he whose turn it was to speak used his
            as an instrument,
took his leather pouch from a pocket
            of his overalls,
gracefully, rubbed tobacco between
            his rough palms
as he set the mood, tamped it into
            the bowl
at a moment carefully chosen, scratched
            a match when it was necessary
to prolong the suspense. If his pipe
            went out it was no accident,
if he spat in the stove it was done
            for a purpose.
When he finished he might lean back
            in his chair so that it stood
on two legs; there'd be a short silence.

The barrens were flat clay fields,
            twenty miles from the sea
and separated from it by dense woods
            and farmlands.
They smelled of salt and the wind
            blew there
constantly as it does on the shore
            of the North Atlantic.

There had been a time, the older men
    said, when someone had owned
the barrens but something had happened
long ago and now anyone who wanted to
    could pasture there.
The cattle ran wild all summer,
sinewy little beasts, ginger-coloured
    with off-white patches,
grazed there on the windswept barrens
    and never saw a human
until fall when the men came to round
    them up,
sinewy men in rubber boots and tweed caps
    with their dogs beside them.

Some of the cattle would by now have
    forgotten
there'd been a time before they'd
    lived on the barrens.
They'd be truly wild, dangerous, the
    men would loose the dogs on them,
mongrel collies, barn dogs with the
    dispositions of convicts
who are set over their fellows,
    the dogs would go for the nose,
sink their teeth in the tender flesh,
    toss the cow on its side,
bleating, hooves flying, but shortly
    tractable.
There were a few escaped,
    it was said, and in a little while
they were like no other cattle—
    the dogs feared them,
they roared at night and the men
    lying by their camp-fires
heard them and moaned in their sleep,
    the next day tracking them
found where they'd pawed the moss,
    where their horns had scraped
bark from the trees—all the stories
    agreed
in this: now there was nothing to do
    but kill them.

14   Land and sea

Old men repeat themselves.
In other words: speak songs.

Can't let the sea be,
the land can't.
                    Won't ever
leave her in peace.
                        Has to keep
troubling the waters,
the land does.
                    This from
Captain Thorburn Greenough
of Hall's Harbour who, in his prime,
could have sailed a bucket
through hell with his handkerchief,
they say.

The land won't let the sea be.

You'd of sailed under
canvas, you'd of knowed that.
Wouldn't of needed me
to tell you.
                    The shore!
We never felt safe
till we was out of her reach.

15   The red wool shirt

I was hanging out my wash,
says the woman in North Sydney.
It was a rope line I was using
and they were wooden pins,
the real old-fashioned kind
that didn't have a spring.

It was good drying weather.

I could see the weir fishermen
at work.
        I had a red wool shirt
in my hands and had just
noticed that one of the buttons
was missing.

Then I looked up and saw
Charlie Sullivan coming
towards me.
He'd always had a funny walk.
It was as if he was walking
sideways.
        That walk of his
always made me smile except
for some reason
I didn't smile
that day.
        He had on a hat
with salmon flies
that he'd tied himself
in the brim.

Poor old Charlie.

It's bad, Mary, he said.

I finished
hanging up the red wool
shirt
        and then I said,
Charlie, it's not
both of them, and he said,
Mary, I'm afraid it is.

And that was that.

I guess he just happened
to be driving past
and when he caught sight
of me kneeling on the grave
must have thought
I was praying or something.

The truth is
I was parting the
white and red wild roses,
irises and raspberry
bushes the better to read
the quaint verse on
the stone above the
two young brothers,
fishermen, who drowned
together, twenty years ago.
Such things interest me.

Now he's asking which one
of the Babcocks am I,
would I be Ernest's boy
or George's eldest?

He grew up with them,
he tells me, and there are
tears in his voice
as he recalls how
he helped lift
their bodies from the Bay.

But they weren't
my father and uncle.
I don't belong here.
I'm nobody.

He takes my hand
in both of his
and waits for me
to say something.

And I wish I were
wearing a mask
or could run away.

17   The Glace Bay cabbies

Each of the cabbies in Glace Bay, Cape Breton,
        has a friend
who rides beside him, all through the night.

They carry on long, intimate, restful
        conversations,
laugh drowsily together, stop
at take-out stands to buy coffee and fish and
        chips
for themselves while the passenger sits
alone in the back seat, under a street-light
        besieged by moths.
They have known each other all their short
        lives,
each driver and his companion, started
        kindergarten
the same day, took jobs in the mines,
were laid off together,
have been driving a taxi ever since,
although only one of them is listed
on the company payroll. They say the same
        things,
more or less, tell each other the same
        stories
every night, he whose turn it is to listen
doing so as attentively as he did the first
        time,
even reminding the other where he was, if
        they've been interrupted:
you were saying such and such, he'll say, and
        the dialogue
will resume at precisely the point where
        it left off.

However, the driver alone addresses the fare
        and this only
when it can't possibly be avoided and in a
        different voice.

Professor, may I introduce you
to two of the Unhappy People, whom you've
        described
as inhabiting a cultural vacuum
somewhere between the swamps of Frustration
and the salt sea of Despair.
May I present my wife's cousins, Corey
        and Brent.
You will note immediately that their teeth
        are translucent,
the colour of reconstituted powdered milk,
which can be attributed to hereditary
        malnutrition,
as their lack of ear-lobes can be ascribed
        to inbreeding.
You are free to make notes, if you wish.
At worst, they'll merely laugh at you.

Professor, I must ask you to forgive
the mandolin, the five-string banjo, the
        guitar, the fiddle
and the jew's-harp. I must ask you to
        bear with
Brent when he dances—he prefers it to
        walking to
the refrigerator for another beer—and
        Corey when he scratches
his groin in symbolic tribute to the girl
        in the yellow bathing suit
playing with a frisbee on the grass across
        the street.
I know it's distracting when, for no
        apparent reason,
they break into song. I can understand
        your not laughing
with them when they talk about driving
four-year-old cars at one hundred and ten
miles per hour down dirt roads with the
        police behind them,
of overturning and wondering drunkenly how
        to shut off
the headlights, until logic triumphed and
        they kicked them out.
I beg you not to be disturbed when they
        whoop

at the tops of their voices—it's in
    their blood,
I'm afraid, their way of declaring an
    instantaneous holiday
and, besides, Brent got out of jail
    this morning
or, as he puts it, got back from his
    annual vacation,
having been locked up this time because
    he didn't
know his own strength, he says, and when
    he was refused service
at the liquor store, being drunk, forgot
    he was carrying
nothing under his left arm to offset
    the force of his right
pushing open the door on his way out
    and so, purely by accident,
drove his fist through the glass:
it could have happened to anybody, Your
    Honour,
he told the Court.
        You must excuse Corey, Professor,
like every member of his family he walks
    in and out
of rooms without thinking it necessary to
    offer
any explanation. When they arrive at my
    house
or any other, they open the door, come in,
    sit down
and, perhaps, switch on the radio. They'd
    expect you to do the same.
If you go to the window, Professor, you'll
    see
that he's talking with the girl in the
    yellow bathing suit
and already has her laughing. "Once you
    got them laughing,
you're as good as in bed with them,"
    Brent says. In celebration
he jumps up again and dances. They've
    brought venison
and wild rice and a half-dozen jars of
    their mother's

homemade preserves and pickles, fresh loaves
    of her bread,
two double cases of beer and a forty-ounce
    bottle
of dark rum, having shut down the cannery
where Corey works in honour of Brent's
    homecoming.
"I said to hell with 'er, let's tie
    'er up,"
and with unanimous approval of his
    fellows,
conveyed without a word, he tied
    her up well
by making certain delicate adjustments
    to the machinery
when the bosses weren't watching. His
    laughter and his brother's
laughter and the laughter of the girl
    in the yellow bathing suit
mingle and rise like water from a
    garden hose, spraying the windows
from inside and out. The passersby turn
and smile, a neighbour's dog runs to see
    what's happening,
a host of starlings take wing, the
    tiger lilies are in flower
at the edge of the parking lot next
    to this house.
Professor, I don't suppose that you'd
    care to arm-wrestle?

From the memoirs of Tom Long

Both times I went Out West
I worked for the same Dutchman.
Drove a team, a horse and a mule.

Other fellows, they liked to
poke fun at me and my mule,
his big ears and all.

But I'll tell you something,
Mister Man:
a mule's got more brains
than a horse. A mule won't eat itself
to death and a horse will.

Never drove much after that.
Father was the teamster,
drove horses all his life.
It was him that told me a horse's eyes
is different than a man's eyes.

Horse thinks a man is fifteen feet tall.
Wasn't for that, horse would take over
             the world.

Luther, the only blind man
in town—which made him a character
in the unfolding chapter
of everybody's private
serialized novel.

Newcomers often went
out of their way to be
kind to him.

The theatre manager,
for instance, picked him up
in his car whenever there was
a change of show and
drove him home afterwards.
(This was before television.)

Other newcomers read him
the papers or listened
very patiently while
he told them the same
boring story for the tenth,
fifteenth or twentieth
time, depending upon
how long it had been
since they'd moved here.

Poor old man! they said
and remarked how little
the locals ever did for him:
some who'd been his neighbours
all their lives
spoke of him with loathing
or told coarse jokes.

In a small town you can
come to know somebody so well
that his eyes can be put out
without this becoming
the central fact
in your relationship.

My wife works beside a woman
who says she's never troubled.
They're packing Easter baskets,
one hundred and forty yesterday,
one hundred and sixty today,
each containing several
hollow chocolate-coconut eggs
and a hollow chocolate-coconut rabbit.

"This place will drive you nuts
if you let it get to you,"
says the woman who is never troubled.
"Me, I don't bother. Two nights a week
I play Bingo, eighteen cards
all at the same time.
Try that and see if it don't
sweep everything else
out of your mind.
It's a lot safer than
running around with men
and a lot cheaper
than getting drunk."

Mickey, our cat, lay under the woodstove.
I'd stretch out on the floor,
legs on cool linoleum, arms on warm tin,
and study her face, knowing if I kept my eyes
          on her
I couldn't help but laugh. It was the
          solemnity
of her expression that tickled me
in the ribs like an uncle's fingers on
          pay-day,
that, and something about the shape of a cat's
          head:
a child will laugh at triangles,
they're such funny circles.

And what laughter! I'd roll over on my back,
kick myself free of the floor and walk on
          the ceiling.
(But only when there were no adults present:
they'd have grabbed me by the shoulders and
          pulled me down.
Don't do that, nobody can walk on the
          ceiling, they'd have said).
I'd walk around the crystal mushroom that
          had been a lamp,
then I'd either walk down the wall
or turn a half-somersault, laughing all
          this time,
change into a horse as easily
as throwing on a coat and gallop out the
          kitchen door.

Nowadays I laugh best at the looking-glass
and it laughs with me, noiselessly. We should
          carry,
each of us, a hand-mirror and when introduced
hold it up, face outwards, laugh with the
          funny fellow
who has lain awake all night and thought
          how terrible
it was that he, of all people, had to die,
who has sat on the side of his bed and almost
          whimpered
not so much because today will end as because
there'll be an end to tomorrows,

not so much for what he'll lose as for what
he can never possess: in other words,
for those uncounted centuries that will
        be held without him,
and who, at last, still seated on his bed,
        has burst out laughing
because what else was there for him to do,
        thinking
how ridiculous it would be if anyone else
felt this way and, then, how ludicrous it was
        that everyone did.

There was a time in between when I never
        laughed,
when nobody does. Adolescents blow
        invisible instruments,
turn their tongues into small hammers
and their teeth into xylophones, run
        barefoot
up and down the keys of an immense
        piano.
But they don't laugh. It's not the same.
Watch closely, listen carefully
and you'll perceive the difference.
It's not something they do when they're
        alone.

If I could turn and meet myself as
        I was then,
gaze into that solemn face, those
        unblinking eyes,
I suppose I'd laugh until I cried,
        then laugh again.

I'm not a good man.
Cars don't trust me
and rightly so:
the fool teaches his
apprentices to fear
making fools of
themselves and
it works for him.

An icy patch ahead
and a snow-bank behind,
me behind the wheel,
cursing like a carpenter
with his thumb in his mouth,
and four nameless men
pushing. Oh, my God,
what if I run over them?
I've never learned
the language in which
they yell instructions.
A car would speak it.

They remind me of
the teamsters of Lunenburg
who used to bellow
at their oxen in
the tongue of their
ancestors or an off-shoot
therefrom, without knowing
it was German,
taking it to be only
the style in which God
had intended men to
address draught cattle.

If I ever spoke to
an automobile it
would hiccough once
and stall
halfway through
an intersection.
I'm not a good man.

Should the car kill one
of them it will be laid to me.
They'd never blame her.
Her! They call the machine
Baby and me nothing.
Come on, Baby, they say.

Oh, and they arch
their backs until
they look scarcely human.
They rock her, they
thrust and thrust again.

I tell them they've
already done more
than enough for me,
remind them they'll
arrive late somewhere,
say to them—and I half
mean this—that, in fact,
it would be rather fun
to stay here the rest
of the night.

I don't matter.
They keep pushing.

They push until
she screeches,
shudders and is freed,

then all but pat her
steaming radiator,
all but whack each other
on the butt like hockey players.

Leaving,
they wave away my thanks.
And so they should.

He was one of those big men
who always look as if their collars
are too tight and their shoes pinch.
This comes from having been
big since birth, I suppose,
from having never fitted in.

I was fifteen, with peach-fuzz
on my upper lip and the legs
of a newborn colt,
as wide-eyed as a kitten,
though I'd not have recognized
myself on the street:
why bother memorizing
a face you'll soon discard?
The very young never know what they
          look like.

Kid that I was, I'd greet him
fondly with a fist in the belly.
Other than that we never touched
nor thought of touching or ever
resolved for any reason not to touch.

We weren't friends. I doubt if a man
          can be
a friend to a boy when in every
          department
where he's not the boy's superior
he's his inferior.

We never once talked of anything
          important.
I laughed in his face, not thinking.
He was Big Alex, who would put up with this
from me, Big Alex my bodyguard
who had nicknamed me Robin.

I gave him nothing
except what he saw in me.
What there was between us
was at once strong and incorporeal
like the scent of lilacs.

He would stare at me sometimes
the way a monk might
stare at the boy Christ.

Last week a farmer I knew by sight
was killed by a bull. Today I'm standing
in a field with thirty of them,
at least fifteen of which are watching me.
They graze for a time, then lift up their heads
and stare as cattle do, with that sorry innocence:
it's as if their species had been
lobotomized and they almost remembered.
Country-bred, I'd have walked among them once
without fear, only respecting their prejudices.
Now I wish there were a fence between us,
mainly because I don't wish to look foolish
and no longer know how cattlemen define prudence.
I'm uncomfortable, and if I were here
for a different purpose I'd be a little afraid.
At work as a journalist, I take on another
identity, become The Man from Maclean's
or Weekend or The Telegraph-Journal.
Headwaiters give me better tables
not because they know who I am but because
I know who I am, don't you see,
and bulls are less apt to gore me.
But to get back to the farmer
who was killed, I'm accompanied by a drover
who's telling me that bulls
are just big kids. They bellow and tussle
but there's no malice in them,
he says, when they drive their horns through
a man or trample him, it's because they don't
realize we're so soft. It's all in fun. He knuckles
one of the yearlings behind the ear.
Nice baby, he says, nice baby. This lad weighs
twelve hundred pounds. Imagine him jumping
into your lap. Nice baby. Playful as a kitten.
Of course, once they start they finish you,
the drover says. Can't blame them for that;
it's the smell of blood that does it.

Our first night here
and I can't sleep
because of the footsteps.
Every house, every
apartment that I've lived
in has made sounds
peculiar to itself
and I've stopped
hearing them after
a week or so, except
when I've been alone
for too long.
The old place on
Parks Street whimpered,
for example. What's that?
guests would ask, some
of them frightened, though
they always laughed.
The ghost of a carpenter
who believed in
cutting corners,
I'd answer.
I'm not sure what
we heard on Brittain Street.
It kept me awake I know,
so it couldn't have been
footsteps. In an apartment
they're nothing. It's different
in a house where you know
everybody's walk and besides
everybody else is asleep.
I suppose the lumber
wasn't properly dried
or the basement leaks.
It won't bother me
much after a night or two.
The old house where I grew up
howled. It would start
in the cellar and before
it reached the attic
the building would be
shaking—I almost said
shaking from head to foot.
I never got used to that.

—for Ian and Bev Cameron

A river of faces
rushing out of
a movie theatre
as we go in:

the faces of
initiates!

Their colour higher
than ours,
they look better-fed and
have permission to smoke.

A hundred of us
know-nothings
shuffle towards
the ticket-takers
while our betters
on the other side
of the long rope
laugh and play with
their car-keys.

They've seen and heard
things we've not.
They know the punch-lines.
They've been given the passwords.

"That old man scares me,"
says an old woman.
It's clear she means me.
I was only fourteen then.

This often happens, the mind
broken loose and floating
in a lake of time.
Somebody should have told me
it wasn't my fault.
But nobody did.

The boy walks with his head down,
kicking pebbles.
This is Visiting Day
with wheelchairs on the lawn,
sunlight on cellophane-
wrapped baskets of soft fruit,
carnations everywhere because
they take so long to die.

When I was in Grade 3
I longed to have an arm
broken so I could wear a sling
or better, much better,
but probably too much
even to hope for,
to be half-blind:
it was the patch I wanted.

Something horrible is
holding on to the boy now:
a skeleton in one of those
flowered frocks
that old women wear.
If I were an old woman
I'd dress like an old man.
I'd refuse to be mocked
with bright colours,
refuse to go out
with my legs and arms
so hideously exposed.

You expected human
bones to be white,
not yellow. This one has claws.
"Take me with you, Daddy," it says.

He wrenches free and walks faster
toward the parking lot
and his father's car.
They'll never drag him here again.

"How can you stand this place?
I can't wait to get home."

The gate man is not unkind.
"I'm afraid you're already there,
old boy," he answers.

Autobiographical note

The poet says, you'll never guess
what happened to me last night.
I made love to the most beautiful
woman in the world.

And the eunuch answers, yeah,
but what good did it do you?
You didn't get paid for it.

*A found poem, taken from
the December 9, 1876, issue
of the Carleton Sentinel,
published at Woodstock, N.B.*

Herman Ott could not get
a living as a carpenter
and consequently became
a grave-digger. This
employment made him
melancholy and he says
he was unable to
repel the idea that
he ought to bury
himself.

      So he dug a grave,
shot himself
at the brink of it
and fell in.

      He had arranged
several bushels
of dirt to fall on him
when his body knocked out
a prop, but
the contrivance did not
work nor did the
bullet kill him.

His physician advises
a change of employment.

35   RCMP raid Cape Breton cockfight

—a recent newspaper headline

Come ye humanitarians
and raise a rousing cheer!
Thanks to the horsemen there'll be no
cockfight at Whitney Pier.

The fancy had laid down their bets,
all set for hellish sport,
when men in spurs kicked in the door
and dragged them off to court.

Some thirty of our feathered friends
were rescued from the pit.
St. Francis of Assisi must
smile when he thinks of it.

There were no crowing champions
that day, no bleeding wrecks.
The civilized and kindly cops
wrung all the roosters' necks.

36   Our exalted brother

A used car salesman may be king and priest
to the dark gods, may wear a sacred chain
and rule that portion of the mystic East
encompassed by the hall on Fifth and Main.

Enthroned, he bids his deacons kiss their swords
and swear that they will give their lives, and more,
to keep the Order's secret grips and words
from infidels beyond this temple's door.

Then, barefoot, led by spearmen and a drum,
the novices, each in a hanged man's hood,
kneel at a torchlit altar and become
for ever brothers of the brotherhood.

He puts aside his chain and occult tome.
They play a little poker and go home.

There's much to be said for taking out
      the telephone.
I tore ours off the wall once and felt
      like a fool
until the event passed into family
      legend.
Since then I've never thought about
      that night
without feeling expansive. The memory
      is enough
to make me invite friends to dinner.
Anyone who has ever torn a telephone
      out by the roots
will know what I mean. It enlarges
      the soul.

But a man who called the company
      and formally requested
that the instrument be removed
      scientifically,
that experts in green uniforms,
      wearing their tool-belts
low on their hips, be sent to
      extract it:
there would be the guest who
      expects to be asked to carve.

38   Here lies

Here lies
Timothy Foley,
born September 26, 1850
at Boston Massachusetts,

Fenian,
soldier of a
half-imaginary Ireland,

he came to help kidnap
Canada
and was shot to death
near this spot

by an unknown member
of the Victoria County
Militia,

thus becoming
the only casualty of
the Battle of Schofield's Farm.

Damn the guide
for grinning when he
tells the tourists this.

39   A certain kind of holy men

Not every wino is a Holy Man.
Oh, but some of them are.
I love those who've learned
        to sit comfortably
for long periods with their hams
        pressed against their calves,
outdoors,
with a wall for a back-rest,
contentedly saying nothing.

These move about only when
        necessary,
on foot, and almost always
        in pairs.
I think of them as oblates.
Christ's blood is in their veins
or they thirst for it.
They have looked into the eyes
        of God,
unprotected by smoked glass.

40   Mr. DeLacey and his guest

The old blind man has welcomed
Baron Frankenstein's hideous creation
into his house.
                    The monster chops wood
while DeLacey teaches him Latin.

But since the cottage consists
of only one small room and a loft
and this is real life
the arrangement can't last

—not with the host playing
his guitar before breakfast
and the guest asking endless
questions about ontogenetics.

My son, in Grade III or IV
and assigned to make a map,
asked us, what colour is
Manitoba? and refused to believe
it didn't matter, provided
it wasn't the same
as Saskatchewan and Ontario.
I remember his face.
I've seldom observed
such constrained rage
except in small children
and university professors.

But it's a common failing,
this excessive faith
in one method of denoting
boundaries. In his atlas
at school, Manitoba was
purple-brown. Similarly,
the road maps indicate
that I live less than
five hundred miles
from my birthplace.

There are truer charts.

I'd never once used
a telephone
in the nineteen years
before I left there,
had never eaten a hamburger;
I could milk a cow by hand
or yoke an ox, knew a man who
once as a passenger
in a heavily-loaded
stage coach inching up
one side of a very steep
hill in California
had got off to walk
and as a result of this
—the downward slope
being equally precipitous,
the horses being compelled
by the weight behind them
to gallop and he having to
run to catch up—

was mistaken by the driver
for a highwayman, and shot:
the scar was still there
after fifty years.
Little else had changed
in our village since
the mid-eighteenth century
when Coulon de Villiers
passed through with his troops,
seven years before
he defeated young George
Washington at Fort Necessity.
Scraps of grape-shot worked
their way to the surface
of the earth the way bits
of shrapnel are said to
emerge at last through the skin
of an old soldier.

Add to all this
that it wasn't the same
for everybody, even there.
My family was poor.
Not disadvantaged—curse
that word of the sniffling
middle classes, suggesting
as it does that there's
nothing worse than
not being like them.
We were poor—curse that word, too,
as a stroke victim
half-maddened by his inability
to utter a certain phrase
will say "shit" instead
and be understood.

A sociologist,
belonging by definition to
one of the lesser
of the ruling sub-castes,
comes from Columbia University
to study a community
in Nova Scotia not very different
from where I was born.
A Tutsi witch doctor among Hutus.
He finds, according to

the New York Times, that
almost everyone he meets is crazy.

It's as if a chemist
had analyzed a river
and declared that its water
was an inferior form of fire.

There are secrets I share
with the very old. I know why
we fought in the Boer War
and how in the lumber camps
we cracked the lice between
our thumbnails and it made
a homely sound, was a restful
occupation of an evening:
cracking lice, we were
like women knitting.

Altogether apart
from that, I bear tribal
marks, ritual mutilations.
My brothers and sisters
fill the slums of every
city in North America.
(God knows this is no boast.)
The poor, whom the Russians
used to call the Dark People,
as if it were in the blood.
I know their footsteps.
We meet each other's eyes.

Don't leave your boots
out there. They'd freeze.
Bring them in where it's warm.

Everyone else is
in the other room
talking with the dead.

I wouldn't joke about
anything like that.

Come see
for yourself.

That's why it took me
so long to answer
your knock.

At first I thought
you were one of them

rapping "yes" or "no,"
which seems to be all
these spirits ever
have to say for themselves.

They're not very clever,
the dead that come to seances.

A boy who's perhaps ten years old
strolls past the Mounties, past the City
        Police,
past the soldiers, past the man from
        Scotland Yard.
What if he were a midget with a gun in
        his pocket?
He hands the Queen something and she
        takes it.
Neither of them smiles. He walks back
        in the crowd.
Nobody else seems to notice this.

The Queen moves on, surrounded by people
who, in a sense, cannot see her
any more than they could see the boy.
What they see is a life-sized,
        three-dimensional,
self-propelled portrait with audio
of a Queen,
           not this woman
who keeps looking down at the object
        in her hand
as if it pleased her but she wasn't sure
what she was expected to do about it.

I suspect that she's asking herself:
Was the boy taking part in a ceremony
with which she's not familiar?
Was there something she failed to do
because her aides forgot to warn her?

She is still carrying the child's gift
        when she gets back in
the Prime Minister's car. Recognizing it
        now, I think to myself
how sad it would have been
for the boy if she had let it drop or
        had passed it
to the man in uniform to whom she passes
        most things
and he had thrown it away at once, as he
        almost certainly would have done,
foolishly thinking a four-leaf clover to be
        of no importance.

I've never before heard a fanfare of
    trumpets
except on television or radio or in
    the movies,
which means that until tonight I've believed
    that
I'd heard a fanfare of trumpets but
    now I know different,
hearing the real thing from the gallery
above me and to my left, with the trumpeters
not bare-legged actors welcoming Moses,
as played by Charlton Heston, home to
    Pharaoh's palace
after conquering Ethiopia,
but members of the Royal Canadian Regiment
    Band
in Boer War scarlet tunics and sun helmets
signalling the arrival of Her Majesty
Elizabeth II, Queen by the Grace of God, and
    all of a sudden,
by God, she is a Queen—which is to say,
    I've been watching
the woman all week and it keeps happening,
this transfiguration: it's as if once
    upon a time
there was this little middle-aged lady
    who'd been sea-sick
all the way from New York and was kept
    awake all night by the fog-horns,
had a backache, an aide said, and whose face
    had that disconnected
look that comes with numb exhaustion,
but this little middle-aged lady had the
    power
to rise several inches into the air and
    float
as she's doing now, and to glow
as if there were a light inside her.

47   The magician and his wife

At first he treated her
as his equal,
the woman he loved,
but this made her weep.

So out of pity he changed her
into a doll
that he works with strings.

Now she sings all day
and smiles at him in her sleep.

One night stand

A woman who's not supposed
to be there has climbed
on the stage.
                    The singer
doesn't know what to do
with her and he's
not what she thought.

They're talking
but we can't hear what
they're saying.
The audience hates this.

Three thousand people
would hurt her if they could.

Until she came along
each of us was alone
with him.

Living in a mad house
is not very different
from living anywhere

although there's a barber's chair
in the bathroom
and no handles on the water-taps

which makes a bent teaspoon
a status symbol: when a man
reaches in his pocket and
takes out his water-key,
purchasable for ten Librium
capsules or fifty books
of matches, it's as if
he'd flipped up the tails
of his tail-coat
and sat down;
no surgeon could be prouder
of washing his hands.

Living in a mad house
is not very different
from living anywhere

although it's good manners
to play bridge after breakfast
and only those who've earned
ground parole are offered
a choice between porridge
and cornflakes:
choosing porridge
would be like refusing
a raise, the attendants would
more than likely report it

to the doctors, whose visits
to the wards are reminiscent
of Old Russia, the Inspector-General
in a white coat with an intern
in a white coat on either side
of him and white-coated orderlies
bringing up the rear,
met by ward attendants
in blue-gray tunics who
would have to move
their heels and elbows

no more than an eighth
of an inch to be
standing at attention.

Living in a mad house
is not very different
from living anywhere.

On Saturdays, the kids
on insulin, go to
the movies downtown,
six or eight of them,
escorted by an attendant
named MacPhee, one of
those unfortunates,
so full of goodwill
that they flutter
like a bird too
well-fed to fly,
whose mere appearance
in a crowd of children
is enough to create
near-anarchy.

It's less than half a mile
from the gate to the theatre
and so they walk there and back,

spreading out, mingling
with the other pedestrians
like a brook joining a river,

having fun with MacPhee
until they stand in the lobby
where, all of a sudden,
they become Those People
from the Asylum.
The word spreads like
a breeze ruffling the grass.

Their revenge is to act
much younger than they are,
to scuffle and giggle
as they file into
the back row seats
reserved for lunatics
and the lights go down.

*Supposedly spoken not by God
but by man, specifically western
man in the last quarter of the
twentieth century.*

Thou shalt not throw a Molotov cocktail
into a public house nor shalt thou lie in wait
for thine enemy at a bus stop, lest
thou meet him face to face.

Thou shalt not go forth alone
against thine enemy, nay, nor in pairs;
in small numbers thou shalt not go forth
    against him.
Thou shalt go forth in armies, thou shalt
    fly
high above his cities and drop eggs of death
on a thousand public houses; thou shalt sit
in an air-conditioned room and thou shalt
    lay thy finger
on a certain button and thereby slay
    thousands
and tens of thousands, nay, millions
    on another continent.

Thou shalt not hold up a train,
instead thou shalt obliterate it, and all
who ride in it, thou shalt shell it from
    the sea;
nor shalt thou take possession
of a school, instead thou shalt send bombers
to rain fire bombs and jellied gasoline
upon many schools. Thou shalt not be a
    terrorist,
in other words,
        thou shalt be a warrior,
for the one is hateful in mine eyes and
    the other glorious.

Election song

Down the street they came with torches
like a roaring human sea,
chanting, "Up with Sir Mackenzie Bowell!
Statesman! Man of Destiny!"

Mackenzie Bowell, Mackenzie Bowell,
may thoughts of your vanished fame
help us keep things in perspective
as we vote for what's-his-name.

The Commonwealth Games open

You're standing in a crowd
of 35,000 people and
they start to sing
a song you've never heard before,
"God Defend New Zealand."

Everybody but you
knows it so well
that no one else
bothers to listen.

I'd call that lonesome.

It's not the same here, the chairman
of the department cautions me.
We're close enough to drive
to Toronto and back
in an evening. Did you know
that in Toronto you can have
the Sunday edition of
the New York Times delivered
to your door the day it comes out?
Life here moves at a faster tempo
than where you are, Down East.
One must adjust to the rhythm
of a different century, one
might almost say.
But you understand that,
I'm sure. Have you been following
this thing in Ethiopia?
A sad business.
I was there
three years ago,
one of a delegation.
We had tea with the Crown Prince,
as he then was.
           A charming fellow
although, obviously, not
the man his father was.
Are you often in Boston?
You'd have no trouble, then,
learning to live with us
in Kitchener.

53   **Ex-Sergeant Whalen tells this story**

The Burgermeister,
                    that's what the Dutch
call their Mayors,
                    Burgermeisters,
the Burgermeister of Nijmegen,
he gave us a big spiel.
                        In English.
I still know some of it
        by heart,
although this was thirty years ago.

The Germans came;
                    we got fed up with them.
The British came
                    and showed us what to do.
The Americans came
                    and told us how great they were.

Then the Canadians came

and so long as they had
        a bottle on the hip
                    and a girl on the arm
they didn't give a damn
                            who
ran the country.

Well!
naturally we gave
                    the Burgermeister
three
cheers
and a tiger.

            But the joke of it was
the Brits and Yanks—
they thought he'd paid
them
        a compliment!

Poor silly buggers,
they cheered too.

Watching him walk toward
the plane I wish it wasn't so easy
to get used to his being here.

It's only when he's leaving
that I remember
this wasn't a homecoming.
He wasn't returning
from a visit, but visiting us.

So that after the first day
or even the first few hours
we didn't say or do
anything special,

when we ought to have
sat up most of the night,
drinking Jamieson's whiskey
out of pewter mugs,
singing Irish songs,
talking,

and got up early
the next morning
to go snowshoeing
in the woods and fry steaks
over a bonfire,

or something like that,
Johnnie, my son,
but I always forget
that you're a guest.

Forgive me, friend,
for I've wounded you.
Look!
        I'll kneel
at your feet,
                like so,
                        and beg.

But you must be quick.
You mustn't hesitate.
You must lift me up
                        now
and not a second later,

or the magic will turn

and I'll despise you
instead of myself.

Doctor Johnson's unfounded fear

Doctor Johnson argued
for an hereditary
aristocracy
on the sensible grounds
that your average Lord
has an average mind.

He believed average minds
deserved to share in
governing the state.

Doctor Johnson feared
that a free electorate
would confer power
only on men of genius.

About twenty-five hours
after you left me, bang,
the door popped open and
this little old woman
in a turquoise dress
slammed herself down in that
big chair by the window
just long enough to say
—this isn't the dressmaker's!

You should have heard her:
it was as if it were my fault.

A trifle, this,
and nothing to cry for.

But I would have told you
when you came home

if you were coming home

and we would have laughed.

57   Not fingers or wool

Now that my hearing
has twice failed me
I understand that
deafness is not
fingers or wool,
although that may be
how it starts.

Strangers
stand at the door
and do not ring,
friends walk in
through the walls,
my wife appears
from out of nowhere.

I am expected
to behave as if this were
commonplace.

And there are times
when others play games:
let's have some
fun with him, they
say to one another, let's
move our mouths and not
make a sound, let's
babble senselessly
in his presence,
let's play
baiting the deaf man.

There are times when
deafness is
believing this.

Oh! says my aunt, not
to me but to my all but
stone-deaf uncle,

neither of them
having seen me
since I was a child
and it so awesome
to be together now:

the three of us have
aged thirty years
this afternoon and
they're far from
convinced I'm who
they've been told;
I only half-believe
they're who they say.

Oh! says my aunt, you're
losing your hearing, are
you, that runs in our
family, we all go
deaf as a post,
sooner or later,
didn't anybody
ever tell you?

Nobody ever did.

What's this, says my
uncle, what's this you
say?
        Deaf!
shouts my aunt,
pointing at me.

Did you say deaf, says
my uncle. I nod. My aunt
nods. It has been
established that we bear
the same mark
in our flesh.

We smile, almost
lovingly, at one another.

59   The boil

Am I alone
         I wonder
in finding pleasure
in this,
       the thumb
and forefinger
rolling tight
          a corner of
the handkerchief,
            then
forcing the spear
of twisted cloth
         under
the ripe core
of the boil
in my own flesh,
            prying it
free,
     burning
the wound clean
with alcohol—
         now
at last
    master
rather than
        servant
of the pain.

The tall, thin man
in the beige topcoat,

who looks to be between
thirty-five and forty
and walks with a slight limp,

is coming out of
a hardware store
where he passed two hundred
dollars in counterfeit
bills: Canadian 20s.

He's visited five
places in ninety
minutes, bought watches,
rings, a sports jacket,
cigarettes and
fishing gear.

A woman and a child
are waiting for him
back at the car

according to the
police radio here
in the newsroom.

Maybe he's whistling.
He doesn't know
that both ends
of the street
are blocked.

That man coming down
while I go up
the airport escalator
—I know him,

open my mouth to speak
before I realize
it's Johnny Carson.

But what's most
surprising is
his facial expression
is the same as mine was:

the eyes seeming to
stare both
outwards and inwards
as the mind stretches
in both directions,
tries to lift an object
out of the past
into the present and
vice versa—this
in the time it takes
to blink.

The moral being:
nobody gets used to
being known by strangers.

Oh, it's not hard
to get used to crowds,
that's another matter,

but meet the eye
of anybody
with recognition
and for that instant
he'll recognize you.

62   Junkets *

You magnificent
redhaired runt!

I wish I could
telephone you
right now
and ask you over.

I've got a new
second-hand pinball
machine.

There's gin.

And we could
send out for
Chinese food,
if you liked.

I don't suppose
you've ever tasted it.

But you're so
far away.
I could never
reach you.

And even if
you were here
in town
I'd be afraid
of intruding:
I'm like that.

Worst of all,
it would never
work,
Junkets:

I'd keep thinking,
dear God,

I'm talking
with John Keats.

*Junkets was a nickname
of John Keats, given
him by Leigh Hunt,
an incorrigible maker
of puns.

Three hundred people,
everyone of them loving me,
that night I read verses.
I don't apologize for this.
I wanted to hug everybody.

Boarding the flight for home,
I smiled at customs officers,
tried to joke with policemen,
inquired after the health
of the stewardesses,

nodded at anyone
who looked me in the eye,
winked at rude children;

if I'd met a snake in the aisle
I'd have stooped to pat it.

Saw my luggage searched
a second and a third time,
was required to show
some identification
other than my ticket,
and was viewed with
universal suspicion:
one child hid his face
in his mother's dress
and blubbered, another
stuck out his tongue at me.

The steward said
I'd have to stop
being so friendly.
The other passengers
were complaining.

That part about
the steward is a lie.
But if I hadn't run out of
love, shortly after take-off,
it might have come to that.

If I live to be a very old man
(and one of my ancestors lived in three
       centuries,
from 1798 to 1902),
I'll probably confuse, terrify or move to
       pity
an adolescent girl, somebody like you,
Elizabeth, by giving her presents she
       finds neither
useful nor enviable nor pretty, things
that would have pleased such a girl
when I was a boy, if I can find them,
a charm bracelet, for instance, though I'd
       rather clothe her
in a skirt that winked mischievously, and
       panties.

You make me think about old age, Elizabeth,
you and the sun that is that bright enough
       that we see
through your blouse and slacks, as we
       ought to.
I think of the aged and ailing King David,
to whose bed, as medicine, the elders brought
       someone like you.
The clods snicker, but what took place then
may have been both sad and wonderful.

Gandhi, too, they say, slept with the young,
only slept with them and, I suppose, woke
       often
as I do who am middle-aged (as we grow older
nothing happens while we're asleep for
       what happens wakes us),
woke often but left her to sleep away the
       night:
it was enough for him that she was there.

This was a form of worship. Oh, Elizabeth,
Elizabeth, Elizabeth, if I were an ancient monarch,
if I were a Hindu sage,
if this were a distant time, another continent,
if we were refugees, if there were no other survivors,
if a ship had sunk and no one else
had reached a life-boat, if you had escaped alone
from a burning cottage and come to me
or, single-handed, had rescued me from an avalanche . . .

Until then it had been such an
        ordinary day,
poached eggs on toast, a morning
        newspaper
that contained no surprises
        (and it's
the unexpected that disturbs us
        most
when we read the papers,
not the merely tragic or horrible),

until then it had been such an
        ordinary day
that, looking back, it seemed to
        him
that he had felt faintly uneasy,
        as though
there was something he was leaving
        out.

A day like any other: you stirred
        the simmering
water to create a whirlpool into
        which you dropped
the eggs, lifted them out with a
        spatula,
dried them carefully over the
        sink; there was war in Africa
and Dagwood Bumstead was hitting
        his neighbour, Herb,
over the head with a baseball bat.

Then it happened—no, then it began to
happen, no, that's not true either, except
in retrospect, for there's no law that says
we have to answer the door or admit whoever
is waiting there (it was like that);
and there were many times in the next
hour when it could have ended
quietly and been forgotten or, in
        the hour following that,
if you'd kept your head you might at
        least have spared
yourself the police, flashbulbs and floodlights,
those gray humanoids filling the pavement
who've come in packs to see.

Probably, he will be a quiet man on weekdays,
employed at one of those jobs where a large number
work more or less alone and there is little
        conversation.
I can picture him sorting letters with a machine
or weighing baggage at an airport;
he gives his superiors no cause to complain;
there is no special reason for anyone to notice him
in the locker room or the cafeteria.

He rides home on the subway or on whatever
        will have replaced it
two or three hundred years from now. (This is
        set in the future).
Occasionally, his name appears in the news
but never prominently. Still, he is the Pope,
        recognized
as Vicar of Christ and successor of St. Peter
by the few thousand Christians that are left,
His Holiness Innocent XIII, and after him
there will come another and another.

Would it be in good taste
to take a picture of Tower Green?

I often ask myself such questions.

The night before
Catherine Howard
was executed
she had them bring
the block to her,
that she might rehearse
dying gracefully.

The act of a Queen, I called it once
—a misjudgment natural to youth.
A true Queen would as lief have winked
at the headsman. Rather, the gesture
of a pert girl (she was twenty-two).

I love you, little Catherine,
and you won't mind my camera.
But it appears that one of the Beefeaters
is furious that I've dared
to desecrate this spot.

He waves both arms,
seems to mouth curses!

I shrink a foot
in height; it's a wonder I don't
slink away on all fours.

Then I understand:
he believes I was swindling him
out of a tip.
                    Life still goes on
in the Tower of London.
I'd forgotten that.

Here is a spiritual descendant
of the warder who carried
the block to the Queen's cell
on the night of February 12th,
fifteen forty-two,

another poor man
with a thankless job to do.

69   If I could be certain, God

If I could be certain, God, that
      you were watching us,
it would be enough. I'd ask less
      of you than an actor
asks of an audience: merely that
      you be there.

You needn't suspend the laws of
      the universe for me.
I'd be embarrassed. And the prospect
      of living for ever
would frighten me almost as much as
      death does.

But if only I could be certain that
      you were watching us
as we, at our best, watch one
      another,
with undemanding affection (now
      I find myself
asking more of you than any actor
      has a right to expect),
but if only I could be certain that
      when the worst happens,
as it will, I won't be alone,
      you'll be there,
you or someone like you, not to
      hold my hand,
not to touch me, not to whisper
      in my ear,
but merely to look on—how splendidly
      I might perform for you!

If I go mad or, rather, say to hell
        with this
and let the crazy man out,
sick and tired of playing Atlas
        to the door
of his closet, of holding it shut
        against him,
I hope he learns how to sew
and can make himself a costume,
preferably of green and gold,
with a mask and a hooded cape.

It would be marvellous if he could
        master
the use of some forgiving weapon,
such as the lasso. I wish he could
        drive
a very fast car or a motorcycle,
painted green and gold. But if I
        go mad
I want this to be real. The car
        and the motorcycle
and, probably, the lasso also
are far more than I dare hope for.

He could laugh differently than
        anyone else
and lose his fear of falling. If
        God is good,
he won't be caught changing his
        clothes
in an alley; there'll be many nights
when he's seen bounding
across the roof-tops, leaping from
one tall building to another,
his cape outspread— the Green Avenger!
And people won't make fun of him,
except nervously, not if God is good.
When his madness kills him,
let it be with a degree of dignity.
Let the onlookers believe
as he does, if only for an instant.

I'm in trouble, she said
to him. That was the first
time in history that anyone
had ever spoken of me.

It was 1932 when she
was just fourteen years old
and men like him
worked all day for
one stinking dollar.

There's quinine, she said.
That's bullshit, he told her.

Then she cried and then
for a long time neither of them
said anything at all and then
their voices kept rising until
they were screaming at each other
and then there was another long silence and then
they began to talk very quietly and at last he said,
well, I guess we'll just have to make the best of it.

While I lay curled up,
my heart beating,
in the darkness inside her.